W9-ARG-908

JAGUARS

BIG CATS

BY TAMMY GAGNE

Consultant: Christina Simmons
San Diego Zoo Global
San Diego, California

CAPSTONE PRESS
a capstone imprint

Edge Books are published by Capstone Press,
1710 Roe Crest Drive, North Mankato, Minnesota 56003.
www.capstonepub.com

Books published by Capstone Press are manufactured with paper
containing at least 10 percent post-consumer waste.

Library of Congress Cataloging-in-Publication Data
Gagne, Tammy.
  Jaguars / by Tammy Gagne.
    p. cm. – (Edge books. Big cats)
  Includes bibliographical references and index.
  ISBN 978-1-4296-7642-7 (library binding)
  1. Jaguar—Juvenile literature. I. Title.
  QL737.C23G345 2012
  599.75'5—dc2   2011010826

Summary: "Describes the history, physical features, and habitat of jaguars" —
Provided by publisher.

Editorial Credits
Brenda Haugen, editor; Kyle Grenz, designer; Svetlana Zhurkin,
    media researcher; Laura Manthe, production specialist

Photo Credits
Alamy: A. & J. Visage, 13, Octavio Campos Salles, 19, Petra Wegner, 20; Ardea:
Nick Gordon, 12, 23; Corbis: Hulton-Deutsch Collection, 27, Jami Tarris,
11, Keren Su, 26, Tom Brakefield, 9; Dreamstime: John Anderson, 10; Getty
Images: Carol Farneti Foster, 18; National Geographic Stock: Frans Lanting,
15, 17; Nature Picture Library: Juan Carlos Munoz, 29, Nick Gordon, 21;
Photolibrary: Gerard Lacz, 22; Shutterstock: Ammit, 1, 14 (bottom), amskad, 16,
Andrew West, 6, Colin Edwards Photography, 25, Darlene Tompkins, 28, Dave
Pusey, 8, ecoventurestravel, 4, Sharon Morris, 7, Stanislav Eduardovich Petrov
(background), throughout, Stayer, cover, Stephen Meese, 5, worldswildlifewonders,
14 (top)

Printed in the United States of America in Stevens Point, Wisconsin.
102011   006404WZS12

TABLE OF CONTENTS

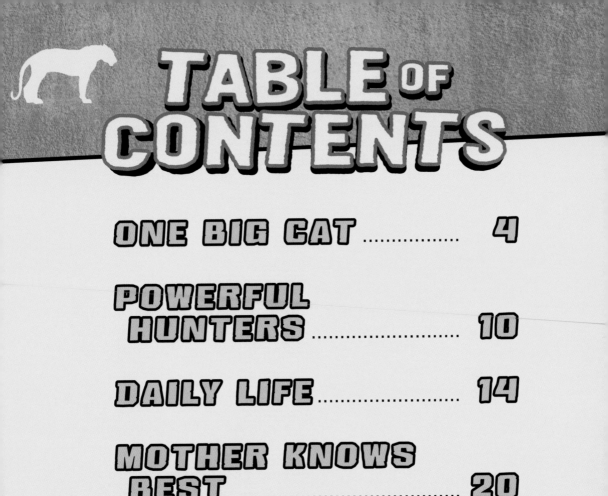

ONE BIG CAT

The rain forest is alive with sounds. Frogs croak, monkeys chatter, and parrots screech. But none of them hears the jaguar. It sits alone in a tree waiting for its **prey**. A white-tailed deer walks quietly below. As soon as the deer takes one more step, the jaguar pounces.

The jaguar is the biggest wildcat west of Africa. It is the third largest cat in the world. Only lions and tigers are bigger than jaguars.

prey—an animal hunted by another animal for food

An adult jaguar's body can measure up to 6 feet (1.8 meters) long. Its tail may add another 30 inches (76 centimeters) to its length. Both males and females have stocky bodies and large heads. Male jaguars weigh between 120 and 300 pounds (54 and 136 kilograms). Females usually weigh about 70 pounds (32 kg).

Jaguars aren't as fast or as tall as the largest cats from Africa and Asia. Jaguars stand between 27 and 30 inches (69 and 76 cm) tall from their shoulders to the ground. These cats rely on their **stealth** and strength for their survival.

Size Comparison Chart

The average height of an American male is 5 feet, 10 inches (178 centimeters).

stealth—the ability to move without being detected

ON THE SPOT

A jaguar's coat has spots. These black marks
appear in clusters on the animal's body. From far
away a jaguar looks like it has many single spots.
Up close you can see that these are actually groups
of spots. Single spots appear only on the animal's
head, legs, and tail.

The base of a jaguar's coat is golden brown or black. Even black jaguars have spots, but you have to look closely to see them.

Big Cat Fact

Some Native Americans believed the jaguar was the god of night, the lord of the underworld.

SHRINKING HOME

Jaguars once lived as far north as Oregon and as far south as northeast Argentina in South America. Today their **range** mainly includes areas of Central and South America. A small number can be found in Arizona and New Mexico.

Many jaguars live in the Amazon rain forest, which is found in the northern part of South America. They can also be found in other **habitats**. Jaguars may live in forests, grasslands, mountain scrub areas, or swamps.

Jaguars have no predators other than humans. They have an average life span of 12 to 15 years. Jaguars kept in zoos can live up to 30 years.

Copycats?

leopard

Jaguars and leopards look a lot alike. Both big cats have golden brown or black fur with black spots. But a leopard has single spots instead of groups of spots. Both cats are also about the same size. But the jaguar has a bigger head and a stockier build. The jaguar also has a shorter, thicker tail. Another difference is where the cats live. Leopards live in Africa and Asia.

range—an area where an animal mostly lives

habitat—the natural place and natural conditions
in which an animal or plant lives

Chapter 2

POWERFUL HUNTERS

Jaguars are mighty hunters. Like most cats, jaguars hunt mostly at night. Jaguars are neither **diurnal** nor **nocturnal**. They sleep whenever and wherever it is safe. And while they prefer to hunt at night, they will hunt whenever the opportunity arises.

These cats have strong jaws and sharp teeth. They usually make a kill in a single bite. Other big cats kill their prey by biting the animal's neck. Jaguars kill by crushing their prey's skull or spine. This powerful bite usually kills the animal instantly.

diurnal—active during the day and resting at night

nocturnal—active at night and resting during the day

Big Cat Fact

Jaguars will travel great distances to find food. They may not be able to outrun their prey, but they can easily overpower it. Jaguars sneak up and jump onto their prey.

Jaguars have strong legs that are useful for climbing. They can climb steep slopes and trees. Sometimes they climb trees and wait to attack their prey from above.

Jaguars almost always hunt alone. The only time jaguars hunt with others is when they teach their cubs. When cubs are learning how to hunt, a mother doesn't always kill the prey. Sometimes she will injure it so the cubs can learn to kill the animal.

11

WHAT'S FOR DINNER?

A jaguar's diet is varied. It eats deer, rabbits, frogs, snakes, and monkeys. It also eats caimans and peccaries. Caimans are similar to alligators. Peccaries are related to wild hogs.

A jaguar's teeth and jaws are strong enough to crush the hardest reptile shells. But a jaguar won't use its teeth to kill smaller animals, such as rodents. It uses its huge paws to crush them instead.

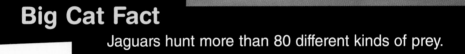

Big Cat Fact

Jaguars hunt more than 80 different kinds of prey.

TIME FOR A SWIM!

Unlike most other cats, jaguars like spending time in water. They are great swimmers. They use their water skills to catch caimans, fish, and turtles in rivers and streams. Jaguars often wave their tails over the water before jumping into it. This movement attracts fish. Jaguars also spend time bathing and playing in the water.

Chapter 3

DAILY LIFE

Jaguars have sharp senses. Using these senses, jaguars can catch prey that few other animals can. For example, caimans have few predators other than the jaguar.

One of a jaguar's best senses is its eyesight. It can see very well at night. Its eyes also adjust quickly to darkness. This **trait** comes in handy when hunting in the forest.

Jaguars are good at judging distances. They use this skill when hunting. They often creep toward their prey before springing on it. A jaguar will wait until it knows the other animal is within reach. Only then will a jaguar leap.

Jaguars also rely on their hearing for locating prey. A jaguar can sense even tiny sounds that its prey makes.

Jaguars also have large paw pads. They walk on their toes. This behavior allows a jaguar to follow prey while hardly making any noise itself.

Smell is important to jaguars too. They use it to sense nearby prey. They also use their noses to pick up the scents of other jaguars.

trait—a quality or characteristic that makes an animal or person different from another

ON THEIR OWN

Jaguars are **solitary** animals. Males live most of their lives alone. Females also live alone when they don't have cubs.

A jaguar's territory is huge. A male jaguar's territory is usually between 19 and 53 square miles (49 and 137 square kilometers). A female's territory is a bit smaller. It usually covers between 10 and 37 square miles (26 and 96 square km).

To keep other jaguars
away, these cats mark their
territory with urine and
feces. Jaguars also claim
territory by clawing trees.
This habit also sharpens
the cats' claws.

MAKING A BIG NOISE

The jaguar is the only cat in North and South America that can roar. It is one of only four big cats in the world that make this sound. Leopards, lions, and tigers also roar. Jaguars can also growl, grunt, and snarl. Neither jaguars nor these other big cats can purr, however.

Big Cat Fact

A jaguar's roar sounds a lot like a loud cough.

Jaguars do not roar when hunting.
They usually roar to scare other
animals away. They will also roar
when defending their territories.
Many other animals back away when
they hear this loud sound.

Chapter 4

MOTHER KNOWS BEST

Male and female jaguars spend only a short amount of time together during mating season. The male goes back to his solitary life before his young are born. He plays no role in raising the cubs.

The female jaguar finds a den when it is time to give birth to her cubs. The place she chooses may be a cave or an area covered by plants. What matters most is that the cubs will be hidden from other animals.

Adult jaguars have no predators, but newborn cubs are defenseless. A mother jaguar will stand up to other animals to protect her cubs. She will even fight adult male jaguars that threaten to kill her cubs. But a mother jaguar must leave her cubs alone when she hunts.

GROWING UP

Female jaguars give birth to between one and four cubs. A jaguar cub weighs between 1.5 and 2 pounds (680 and 907 grams) at birth. Its eyes are closed for about the first week of its life. A cub depends on its mother for everything.

Female jaguars nurse their cubs for about 5 months. Mother jaguars also **regurgitate** meat for their young. This starts when the cubs are about 2 weeks old. Eating this meat is a cub's first step toward eating solid food.

Cubs remain with their mother for about a year and a half. She teaches them how to survive. A mother teaches cubs how to hunt on land and in water. She also shows them how to climb trees and wait for prey.

regurgitate—to vomit food after it has been eaten

MOVING ON

When the cubs are ready, they leave their mothers. Males often stay close to each other as they move into adulthood. Brothers may even live and hunt together for a few months. Then they go off in search of their own territories farther away.

Female jaguars also find their own territories. But the females usually don't wander too far from their mothers. Sometimes a female jaguar will take over her mother's territory. In this case the mother often settles in a neighboring area.

Some young adults return to the area where they were born shortly after leaving it. When this happens, they may remain with their mothers as long as a month or more. They then move on without returning again.

Chapter 5

AT RISK

Jaguars are **endangered**. This means that they are at risk of becoming **extinct**. No one knows exactly how many jaguars live in the wild.

Jaguars have no predators other than people. People living in Central and South America have long hunted these big cats for their fur. Coats made from jaguar fur have sold for thousands of dollars. Problems began when demand for jaguar coats spread to the rest of the world.

A Continuing Problem

A great deal of hunting in the 1960s decreased jaguar populations quickly. Today it is illegal to sell the cats' skins in many countries. But some people continue to hunt jaguars and sell their skins.

A hunter in the 1930s stands by the skins of jaguars he has killed.

endangered—at risk of dying out

extinct—no longer living; an extinct animal is one that has died out, with no more of its kind

Big Cat Fact

Since 1900 the jaguar has lost more than half of its range. Reasons include habitat loss and decreases in prey populations.

OTHER ISSUES

Some jaguars wander onto farmland. They will eat cows, horses, and sheep if they can get to them. Ranchers often kill jaguars to keep their livestock from being attacked.

The reason many jaguars attack farm animals is because of habitat loss. People are taking more and more of the jaguar's territory for farmland.

Conservation groups are helping ranchers protect their livestock without killing jaguars. Guard dogs and electric fences can keep the jaguars away from farm animals. Some farmers even set off fireworks to keep the jaguars away.

Jaguars need protection because they play an important part in the environment. They help keep nature in balance by eating prey animals.

The jaguar reserve in Pantanal National Park in Brazil

RESERVA ECOLOGICA DO JAGUAR

Reserva Particular do Patrimônio Natural (R.P.P.N.)

"Pantaneiros Preservando o Pantanal"

Patrocínio:

BLACK DIAMOND
P A V I N G

www.FocusTours.com   www.BlackDiamondPaving.com   www.FocusConservation.org

GLOSSARY

diurnal (dye-UR-nuhl)—active during the day and resting at night

endangered (in-DAYN-juhrd)—at risk of dying out

extinct (ik-STINGKT)—no longer living; an extinct animal is one that has died out, with no more of its kind

habitat (HAB-uh-tat)—the natural place and conditions in which an animal or plant lives

nocturnal (nok-TUR-nuhl)—active at night and resting during the day

prey (PRAY)—an animal hunted by another animal for food

range (RAYNJ)—an area where an animal mostly lives

regurgitate (ree-GUR-juh-tate)—to vomit food after it has been eaten

solitary (SOL-i-terr-ee)—living alone

stealth (STELTH)—the ability to move without being detected

trait (TRATE)—a quality or characteristic that makes an animal or person different from another

READ MORE

Carney, Elizabeth. *National Geographic Kids. Everything Big Cats.* Washington, D.C.: National Geographic, 2011.

Dorisi-Winget, Dianna. *Snow Leopards.* Big Cats. Mankato, Minn.: Capstone Press, 2012.

Walker, Sally M. *Jaguars.* Nature Watch. Minneapolis: Lerner Publications, 2009.

INTERNET SITES

FactHound offers a safe, fun way to find Internet sites related to this book. All of the sites on FactHound have been researched by our staff.

Here's all you do:

Visit *www.facthound.com*

Type in this code: 9781429676427

Check out projects, games and lots more at
www.capstonekids.com

INDEX